MAR 21

D1716617

EXPLORE THE WORLD

THE GEOGRAPHY OF THE UNITED STATES AND CANADA

JILL KEPPELER

PowerKiDS press.

New York

Published in 2021 by The Rosen Publishing Group, Inc.
29 East 21st Street, New York, NY 10010

First Edition

Editor: Caitie McAneney
Book Design: Tanya Dellaccio

Photo Credits: Cover Harold Stiver/EyeEm/Getty Images; series background MicroOne/Shutterstock.com; p. 5 MicroOne/Lonely Planet Images/Getty Images Plus/Getty Images; p. 6 LesPalenik/Shutterstock.com; p. 7 Patrick Poendl/Shutterstock.com; p. 9 (map) https://upload.wikimedia.org/wikipedia/commons/3/34/Us_population_2005_lrg.jpg; p. 9 (Toronto) Stephane Legrand/Shutterstock.com; p. 10 The Washington Post/Getty Images; p. 11 Angel McNall Photography/Shutterstock.com; p. 13 (top) Sean Pavone/Shutterstock.com; p. 13 (bottom) Archive Photos/Getty Images; p. 15 MarkVanDykePhotography/Shutterstock.com; p. 16 Stock Montage/Archive Photos/Getty Images; p. 17 Posnov /Moment/Getty Images; p. 19 Gary Ives/Shutterstock.com; p. 21 (maps) Ink Drop/Shutterstock.com; p. 21 (New York City) J2R/Shutterstock.com; p. 23 (top) Rainer Lesniewski/Shutterstock.com; p. 23 (bottom) Dan Thornberg/EyeEm/Getty Images; p. 25 Nancy Anderson/Shutterstock.com; p. 27 cestes001/iStock/Getty Images; p. 29 Bryan Mullennix/EyeEm/Getty Images.

Cataloging-in-Publication Data
Names: Keppeler, Jill.
Title: The geography of the United States and Canada / Jill Keppeler.
Description: New York : PowerKids Press, 2021. | Series: Explore the world | Includes glossary and index.
Identifiers: ISBN 9781725321885 (pbk.) | ISBN 9781725321908 (library bound) | ISBN 9781725321892 (6 pack) | ISBN 9781725321915 (ebook)
Subjects: LCSH: North America–Juvenile literature. | North America–Geography–Juvenile literature.
Classification: LCC E38.5 K47 2020 | DDC 917–dc23

Manufactured in the United States of America

CPSIA Compliance Information: Batch #CSPK20: For Further Information contact Rosen Publishing, New York, New York at 1-800-237-9932

Find us on

CONTENTS

FROM THE MOUNTAINS TO THE PRAIRIES

Perhaps the most notable geographic trait of the United States and Canada, the two countries that make up the majority of the continent of North America, is that there isn't a single trait. Their shared area is marked by huge variety in landforms and other physical characteristics, climate, and **precipitation**.

This variety has affected the origin, development, and economies of both countries. The richness of the land's resources has made the United States and Canada two of the wealthiest countries in the world. They have other things in common as well, including a **democratic** background, language, and many aspects of culture.

From tall mountains to sprawling plains and from wet rain forests to dry deserts, the geography of these two countries **encompasses** all the major types of **biomes** in the world.

A STATE APART

Two U.S. states are separated geographically from the rest of the country. Alaska is at the far northwestern part of North America. Hawaii, however, is in the middle of the central Pacific Ocean. It's made up of eight major islands and more than 100 islets, or small islands. The islands are volcanic, and there's still a lot of volcanic activity in Hawaii today. Mauna Loa on the main island of Hawaii is the world's largest volcano.

THINK LIKE A GEOGRAPHER

THE UNITED STATES AND CANADA AREN'T THE ONLY COUNTRIES THAT MAKE UP NORTH AMERICA. GREENLAND, MEXICO, AND MANY OTHER SMALLER COUNTRIES ARE CONSIDERED PART OF THE CONTINENT.

Though they're two different countries, the United States and Canada can both claim one notable landmark: Niagara Falls.

5

OLD ROCKS, RICH RESOURCES

North America is made up of some of the oldest rocks on Earth. The continent was built up on a continental shield called the Canadian (or Laurentian) Shield, which is huge—about 3 million square miles (7.8 million sq km). The shield is centered on Canada's Hudson Bay. It's the biggest chunk of exposed **Precambrian** rock on Earth.

While much of the shield is exposed across Canada, it's mostly covered by sedimentary rock in the United States—except for a few areas, including the Adirondack Mountains. The Appalachian Mountains stand to the southeast of the shield, and the ranges that include the Rocky Mountains, the Sierra Nevadas, and others stand to the west. The Great Plains and other lowlands lie between them.

THINK LIKE A GEOGRAPHER

A CONTINENTAL SHIELD IS A HUGE, STABLE, LOW AREA IN EARTH'S CRUST. SHIELDS ARE MADE OF PRECAMBRIAN ROCKS THAT CAN BE ANYWHERE FROM 540 MILLION TO 3 BILLION YEARS OLD.

Thousands of millions of years ago, glaciers smoothed much of the rock of the Canadian Shield. They left behind rocky hills and basins that are now often lakes or swamps.

THE CORDILLERA

A cordillera is a system of mountain ranges arranged in somewhat parallel chains. The mountain ranges that rise to the west of the Canadian Shield are sometimes called the Cordillera or Cordilleras. They take up about a third of the land in the United States. They include the Rocky Mountains in the eastern part of the ranges, the Coast Ranges and the Klamath Mountains on the West Coast, and the Sierra Nevadas and the Cascade Range in the middle.

The United States and Canada have many natural resources, in part due to their great variety of landforms. There are valuable minerals underground and the soil in many locations is very fertile, or rich. There are also many forests and sources of fresh water. These resources have made the countries two of the wealthiest in the world.

The overall area of the United States is about 3.8 million square miles (9.8 million sq km)—just about the same as that of Canada. However, their populations differ greatly. The United States has about 327 million people, while Canada has about 37 million.

The United States and Canada share a border that's more than 5,500 miles (8,851.4 km) long. It's the longest border in the world that isn't patrolled by the countries' military.

WHY SO SMALL?

Canada is one of the world's biggest countries by landmass, but it has the 39th biggest population, most of which lives in a very small area. The Toronto metropolitan area alone has 6.1 million people—about 17 percent of the country's total population. This population divide has to do, in part, with the climate. The northern areas of Canada are very cold and snowy, and most agriculture developed in the south.

THINK LIKE A GEOGRAPHER

MOST OF THE PEOPLE IN CANADA LIVE WITHIN 185 MILES (297.7 KM) OF THE U.S. BORDER.

CANADA

UNITED STATES

POPULATION DENSITY 2005

- 10+ PEOPLE
- 100+ PEOPLE
- 1,000+ PEOPLE

Toronto, Canada's biggest city, is located in the province of Ontario. Canada is divided into provinces in a similar way the United States is divided into states.

9

FIRST PEOPLES

No one is exactly certain when the first people came to North America. Right now, many scientists think that Stone Age hunters from northeastern Siberia crossed (perhaps on a land bridge) to Alaska about 20,000 years ago. Some scientists even claim they arrived much sooner. From there, the hunters moved throughout the continent. These travelers were the ancestors of the **indigenous** peoples of the United States and Canada today.

Geography had a lot to do with how these early residents spread out in North America. They most likely followed a somewhat ice-free path from Alaska and then were able to spread out across an enormous continent. Because of the size of the area, there may have been relatively little contact between groups, some of which began, in time, to build settlements and practice agriculture.

THINK LIKE A GEOGRAPHER

AMERICAN INDIANS SOMETIMES BUILT CITIES, SUCH AS THE CAHOKIA MOUNDS SITE IN THE CURRENT STATE OF ILLINOIS. AS MANY AS 20,000 PEOPLE MAY HAVE LIVED THERE AT ONE POINT.

The Pueblo Indians in the U.S. Southwest built homes of adobe and stone, while peoples in the Northeast used trees to build. Each group used what was available in their area.

MANY CULTURES, MANY PEOPLES

There were (and are) many different groups, traditions, and cultures among these first people of North America. Some people tend to believe that "American Indian" means one big culture. This isn't true. The term encompasses many different peoples with many different ways of life, often affected by where they settled. For example, those who settled along the Pacific coast used the ocean for many resources, while those who settled on the plains often followed the herds of bison.

NEWCOMERS AND INVADERS

Around 1500, an influx of newcomers to North America would change everything, both for the physical geography and the population of the continent. European explorers began to "discover" the Americas, and huge numbers of people from that area began to travel to the so-called "New World." These invaders saw the continent as a wilderness to be tamed and developed, with a relatively small population of natives that hadn't (by their standards) taken full advantage of the land, including its forests, grasslands, and mineral resources. Therefore, they thought they had the right to do so.

The newcomers enslaved and killed many of the native peoples. Even more died because of diseases the invaders brought with them. Within 100 years or so, about 90 percent of the native population in North America had died.

IMPORTED IDEAS

The Europeans influenced the area that they called "The New World" in many ways. They brought their own languages, especially English and French, their Christian religion, and their types of government. The settlers in the original British colonies set up new systems of government, which grew into a kind of **limited government**. They founded the Jamestown colony in 1607 in Virginia, and from there, the colonies began to grow.

THINK LIKE A GEOGRAPHER

THE EUROPEAN NEWCOMERS CHANGED THE LANDSCAPE OF THE CONTINENT SO MUCH IN PLACES THAT IT'S HARD TO EVEN GUESS ABOUT WHAT IT WAS LIKE BEFORE THEIR ARRIVAL.

Saint Augustine, the first permanent European settlement in what came to be the United States, has been part of the country since 1821. Many people visit its old buildings and museums.

LIMITED GOVERNMENT: IN A LIMITED GOVERNMENT LED BY THE CITIZENS, EVERYONE, INCLUDING ALL AUTHORITY FIGURES, MUST OBEY THE LAWS.

13

UNITED WE STAND

Today's United States started with the 13 British colonies, and it ranged down the East Coast. The geography and resources of this area, between the Atlantic Ocean and the Appalachian Mountains, included rich soil, many trees, and plentiful animals. The soil was excellent for crops such as tobacco, indigo, and rice, which made some colonial landowners very rich. The amount of land available brought many immigrants to the continent.

After the colonies earned their independence from Great Britain in the American Revolution and became the United States, they started expanding westward. They spread over the Appalachian Mountains and then across the Mississippi River in a great **migration**. They settled in lands that then belonged to Mexico. In time, the nation spread from coast to coast, plus Alaska and Hawaii.

THE IMPACT OF SLAVERY

Many Europeans settled in what would become the United States, but they weren't the only group. Starting in 1619, they brought captive Africans to be used as slaves on large farms and plantations. The number of slaves grew as more Europeans arrived, bringing nearly 12.5 million black slaves to the New World, with 388,000 transported to North America. These captives brought their own cultures and beliefs along with them as well. Today, African Americans make up a least 12 percent of the U.S. population.

THE TALL APPALACHIAN MOUNTAINS KEPT THE EARLY UNITED STATES AND CANADA FROM EXPANDING WESTWARD AT FIRST. SOME OF THE GEOGRAPHY OF THE GROWING COUNTRIES WAS SO ROUGH THAT IT INFLUENCED SETTLERS' IMAGE OF THEMSELVES AS A TOUGH PEOPLE.

The Appalachian Mountains are a natural barrier between parts of the United States: the interior lowlands and the eastern coastal plain. Because of this, they've had a great effect on how the nation developed.

MIGRATION: MOVEMENT FROM ONE REGION TO ANOTHER.

OH, CANADA!

The rich resources in the future Canada drew the first European settlers there. They created an active fur trade and many fisheries. For many years, Great Britain and France fought over land in the region, culminating in the Seven Years' War starting in 1756. In 1759, the British won a decisive battle over the French near Quebec City, and France gave up most of its North American land to Great Britain.

In 1867, the British **Parliament** passed the British North America Act, giving Canada (then divided into the provinces of Ontario and Quebec), New Brunswick, and Nova Scotia their own government and naming the collective region "the **Dominion** of Canada." The colonies of Prince Edward Island and British Columbia soon joined the dominion as well, and others followed.

THINK LIKE A GEOGRAPHER

CANADA GOT ITS NAME WHEN EXPLORER JACQUES CARTIER (WHO CLAIMED THE REGION FOR FRANCE IN THE MID-1500S) HEARD NATIVE PEOPLES USE THE IROQUOIS WORD *KANATA*, WHICH MEANS "VILLAGE."

L'ANSE AUX MEADOWS

The Norse actually reached North America long before the British, French, or Spanish did. About AD 1000, Norse explorers created a settlement at the northern part of what would become Newfoundland and Labrador. This base was later abandoned, perhaps because it was so far away from Norway. Today, the site [now called L'Anse aux Meadows] is a World Heritage Site. Tourists can visit and see restored Viking homes and many exhibits.

STATES AND PROVINCES

Today, the United States is divided into 50 states and the District of Columbia. The original 13 states are those that went to war with Great Britain in 1776 to earn independence, while Alaska and Hawaii became the newest two states in 1959. In 1912, Arizona became the last state in the **contiguous** United States to join the country. There are also 14 U.S. territories, only five of which are permanently inhabited. These are Puerto Rico, Guam, the U.S. Virgin Islands, the Northern Mariana Islands, and American Samoa.

Canada, on the other hand, is divided into 10 provinces. The provinces are Alberta, British Columbia, Manitoba, New Brunswick, Newfoundland and Labrador, Nova Scotia, Ontario, Prince Edward Island, Quebec, and Saskatchewan. It also has three territories, which are the Northwest Territories, Nunavut, and Yukon.

BY THE NUMBERS

In the United States, California has the biggest population: nearly 40 million people. Wyoming has the smallest population: less than 600,000 people. However, California is the third largest state by landmass, while Wyoming is the ninth largest. Rhode Island is the smallest state by landmass: only about 1,034 square miles [2,678 sq km]. In Canada, Quebec is the largest province by landmass [and the second biggest after Ontario by population] and Prince Edward Island is the smallest in both respects.

Residents of most of the U.S. territories [except for American Samoa] are U.S. citizens. Puerto Rico, shown, is a **commonwealth** of the United States.

THINK LIKE A GEOGRAPHER

THE GRAND CANYON, AN AMAZING LANDFORM CUT INTO THE EARTH BY THE COLORADO RIVER OVER MILLIONS OF YEARS, IS LOCATED IN THE U.S. STATE OF ARIZONA. MANY PEOPLE VISIT IT EVERY YEAR.

19

URBAN AREAS

New York City, located in New York State, is the most populated city in the United States, with about 8.6 million people. The city became so large and so important in large part because of its geography. It sits right where the Hudson and East Rivers reach New York Harbor, one of the most-used ports in the world. Its role as an **immigration** hub also helped.

Toronto is Canada's most populated city for many of the same reasons. The city sits right on the shore of Lake Ontario, one of the North American Great Lakes, and has a natural harbor and easy access to the Saint Lawrence Seaway for trade and shipping. **Urban** areas in the United States and Canada are often **multicultural**, connecting people from all over the world.

THINK LIKE A GEOGRAPHER

THE SECOND MOST POPULATED CITY IN THE UNITED STATES IS LOS ANGELES, CALIFORNIA, ON THE WEST COAST. ABOUT 4 MILLION PEOPLE LIVE IN ITS METROPOLITAN AREA. THE SECOND MOST POPULATED CITY IN CANADA IS MONTREAL, WITH ABOUT 3.5 MILLION PEOPLE.

MULTICULTURAL: HAVING MANY DIFFERENT CULTURES, OR WAYS OF LIFE OF DIFFERENT PEOPLES, IN A UNIFIED SOCIETY.

MEXICAN CULTURE IN THE UNITED STATES

At the end of the U.S.-Mexican War in the 1840s, the two countries signed a treaty that gave the United States a great deal of land in what used to be Mexico. Thousands of Mexicans became U.S. citizens without even moving, adding their cultures [and their use of Spanish] to the United States. Later, industries in the United States drew many Mexican workers. Immigration from Mexico continues today, keeping the two neighboring countries connected.

NEW YORK CITY

TORONTO

Both Toronto and New York City, shown, are very multicultural cities.

21

WATERS OF NORTH AMERICA

Not only do the United States and Canada have many ocean shores, they have many huge rivers, large lakes, and other freshwater resources. The Mississippi River, one of the longest rivers in the world, cuts across the United States roughly from north to south. The continent's many rivers and their routes made it easier for people who originally settled on the East Coast to travel into the interior of the continent.

The lakes of North America also had (and have) a big impact on the countries. The five Great Lakes of the eastern part of the continent have affected settlement, trade, travel, recreation, and fishing, as have the nations' many smaller lakes. The United States and Canada have eight of the 15 largest lakes in the world.

THINK LIKE A GEOGRAPHER

WATERWAYS WERE SO IMPORTANT TO THE DEVELOPMENT OF THE UNITED STATES THAT PEOPLE STARTED BUILDING THEM IN THE FORM OF CANALS, SUCH AS THE ERIE CANAL.

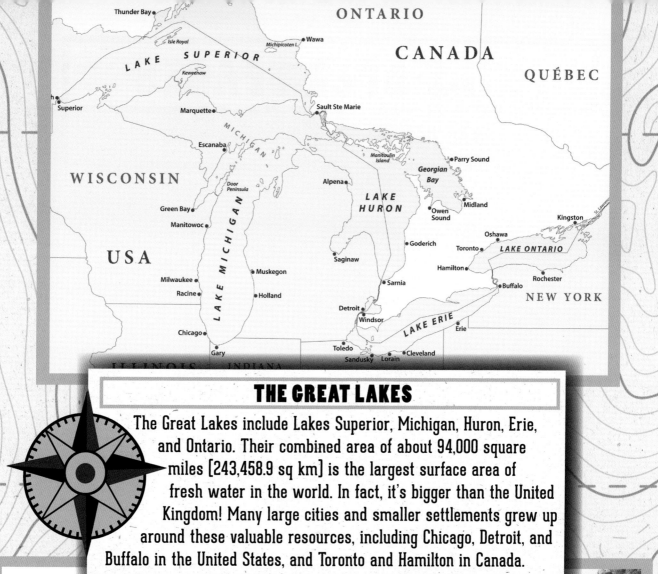

THE GREAT LAKES

The Great Lakes include Lakes Superior, Michigan, Huron, Erie, and Ontario. Their combined area of about 94,000 square miles [243,458.9 sq km] is the largest surface area of fresh water in the world. In fact, it's bigger than the United Kingdom! Many large cities and smaller settlements grew up around these valuable resources, including Chicago, Detroit, and Buffalo in the United States, and Toronto and Hamilton in Canada.

The Mississippi River is part of the drainage system for all or part of two Canadian provinces and 31 U.S. states.

WIDE-OPEN SPACES

While mountains greatly affected the human geography of the United States and Canada, the two countries also have many lowlands and plains. In Canada, the Canadian Shield is surrounded by lowlands. The Great Lakes-Saint Lawrence lowlands in southern Ontario include very fertile areas, as do the country's interior plains. Mineral resources are also plentiful.

The center of the United States is mostly one huge series of lowlands. They run between mountains to the east and west, although there's also a coastal plain that runs down the east and south. The enormous Great Plains are part of the interior lowlands, making up about a third of the country (and part of Canada as well). It's largely agricultural territory, even today.

THE BREADBASKETS

A "breadbasket" is a region in which much of the world's food [often grains in particular] is grown. The Canadian prairies, including the provinces of Alberta, Manitoba, and Saskatchewan, are considered a breadbasket. San Joaquin Valley in California and the states of the so-called U.S. heartland, or the very center of the country, are also considered breadbaskets. However, scientists are concerned that climate change caused by humans could destroy many of the world's breadbaskets in coming years, including those in North America.

SOME OF THE GREAT PLAINS STATES ARE THE LEAST **DENSELY** POPULATED CONTINENTAL STATES IN THE UNITED STATES: WYOMING, MONTANA, NORTH DAKOTA, AND SOUTH DAKOTA.

Saskatchewan alone exported more than $11 billion worth of wheat and other produce in 2012.

A DIVERSITY OF DISASTERS

Although the United States and Canada have many natural resources that attracted explorers, traders, and immigrants, both countries deal with natural disasters of various kinds. They're both so large and so **diverse** in land types and climates that different regions experience different issues. **Avalanches**, blizzards, **hurricanes**, floods, landslides, tornadoes, and wildfires can all be problems in different locations.

California is well known for its earthquakes, thanks to the San Andreas Fault, but earthquakes are also possible in other states and Canada. Hurricanes are most often considered an issue for the Gulf and Atlantic coasts, but they can reach inland more than many people realize. Tornadoes plague the midwestern states and the Great Plains, but they may also happen in other areas.

THINK LIKE A GEOGRAPHER

THE 1906 SAN FRANCISCO EARTHQUAKE (AND THE FIRES IT CAUSED) KILLED ABOUT 3,000 PEOPLE. IT'S CONSIDERED THE UNITED STATES' SECOND MOST DEADLY NATURAL DISASTER.

DIVERSE: DIFFERENT OR VARIED.

DEADLY STORMS

The two most deadly natural disasters to take place in the United States and Canada were both hurricanes. On September 9, 1775, a hurricane hit the island of Newfoundland in Canada, destroying fishing boats, flooding the shore, and killing 4,000 people. Nearly 125 years later to the day, on September 8, 1900, a hurricane hit Galveston, Texas, killing 8,000 to 9,000 people and nearly destroying the entire city. Neither of these tolls has been surpassed.

Hurricane Maria, which hit the U.S. commonwealth of Puerto Rico in 2017, may have killed more than 4,000 people, but there's no official death toll from the government. It could be the second deadliest U.S. natural disaster.

IN THE FUTURE

The basic geographies of the United States and Canada have been more or less stable for years now, but change is always on the horizon. Some regions will grow in population, while others will lose people to those other regions. Climate change may continue to make weather patterns and natural disasters worse throughout the continent. A drive for sustainability, or living in a way that doesn't use up natural resources, may make a difference as well.

The United States and Canada are two of the most diverse countries in the world, both in terms of their people and their physical geography. If the people of these countries take care of all those resources, this region will continue to prosper for years to come.

CLIMATE CRISIS

Scientists say that, due to climate change, shifting climate zones in North America could cause many cities to find themselves with a whole new climate within one generation. Northern cities will have the climates of southern cities, and southern cities will grow even warmer than they are. This could affect precipitation, many natural resources, natural disasters such as drought and wildfires, and even the physical geography of the continent.

THINK LIKE A GEOGRAPHER

A RISE IN SEA LEVELS DUE TO CLIMATE CHANGE COULD AFFECT ISLANDS IN NORTH AMERICA AND MANY COASTAL AREAS.

By 2080, the city of Calgary in Alberta, Canada, could have a climate more like a city in South Dakota, both warmer and wetter.

GLOSSARY

avalanche: A large mass of snow sliding down a mountain or over a cliff.

biome: A natural community of plants and animals, such as a forest or desert.

commonwealth: An area much like a U.S. state but that pays no federal taxes and that has a representative in Congress who does not vote.

contiguous: Touching each other or immediately next to each other.

democratic: Treating everyone as equals; describing a form of government in which all citizens participate.

dense: Having parts that are close together.

Dominion: A country that was part of the British empire but has its own government.

encompass: To include something as a part.

hurricane: A powerful storm that forms over water and causes heavy rainfall and high winds.

immigration: The act of coming to a country to settle there.

Parliament: The law-making body of England, now the United Kingdom.

Precambrian: Relating to the earliest era of geological history.

precipitation: Rain, snow, sleet, or hail.

urban: Relating to a city.

FOR MORE INFORMATION

BOOKS

DK. *Timelines of Everything.* London: Dorling Kindersley Limited, 2018.

Moore, Christopher. *The Big Book of Canada: Exploring the Provinces and Territories.* Toronto, Ontario: Tundra Books, 2017.

National Geographic Kids. *National Geographic Kids United States Atlas.* Washington, D.C.: National Geographic, 2017.

WEBSITES

North America: Physical Geography

www.nationalgeographic.org/encyclopedia/north-america-physical-geography

Take a peek at the varied geography of North America through maps and thorough information.

U.S. States

kids.nationalgeographic.com/explore/states

Get a fascinating look at the 50 U.S. states through facts and photos.

Where Is the Great White North?

www.wonderopolis.org/wonder/where-is-the-great-white-north

Learn about Canada through trivia and videos.

INDEX